8/15
YA
006.754
Greek

Grant Area District Library
122 Elder Street
Grant, Michigan 49327

A TEEN'S GUIDE TO THE POWER OF SOCIAL NETWORKING™

SOCIAL NETWORK–POWERED INFORMATION SHARING

JOE GREEK

New York

Published in 2014 by The Rosen Publishing Group, Inc.
29 East 21st Street, New York, NY 10010

Copyright © 2014 by The Rosen Publishing Group, Inc.

First Edition

All rights reserved. No part of this book may be reproduced in any form without permission in writing from the publisher, except by a reviewer.

Library of Congress Cataloging-in-Publication Data

Greek, Joe.
Social network–powered information sharing/Joe Greek.
 pages cm—(A teen's guide to the power of social networking)
Includes bibliographical references and index.
ISBN 978-1-4777-1681-6 (library binding)—
ISBN 978-1-4777-1915-2 (pbk.)—
ISBN 978-1-4777-1916-9 (6-pack)
1. Online social networks. 2. Information society—Social aspects. 3. Information technology—Social aspects. I. Title.
HM742.G74 2013
006.7'54—dc23

2013013757

Manufactured in Malaysia

CPSIA Compliance Information: Batch #W14YA: For further information, contact Rosen Publishing, New York, New York, at 1-800-237-9932.

CONTENTS

INTRODUCTION 4

CHAPTER 1
THE SOCIAL INFORMATION AGE 8

CHAPTER 2
TRACKING THE LOCAL SCENE 19

CHAPTER 3
INFORMATION SHARING'S IMPACT UPON JOURNALISM, PUBLIC HEALTH, AND PUBLIC DEBATES 33

CHAPTER 4
THE GLOBAL TOWN SQUARE 44

CHAPTER 5
SAFE INFORMATION SHARING-TODAY AND TOMORROW 57

GLOSSARY 69
FOR MORE INFORMATION 71
FOR FURTHER READING 73
BIBLIOGRAPHY 75
INDEX 78

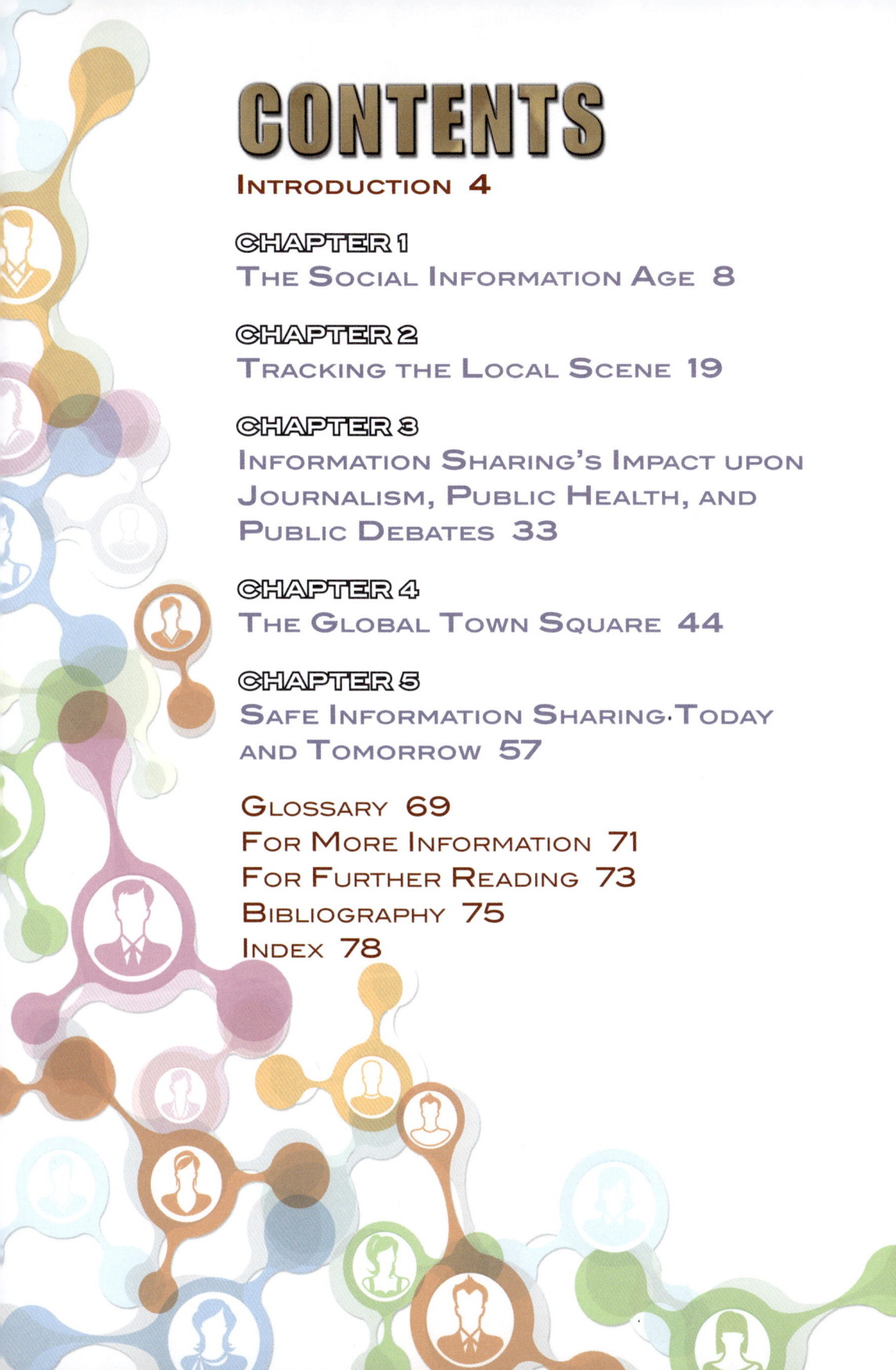

INTRODUCTION

By the end of 2012, the number of people with a Facebook account surpassed the one billion mark. An estimated 618 million of those individuals visited the social networking Web site on a daily basis. According to projections by the U.S. Census Bureau, the world population for the same year topped seven billion. In other words, close to one in seven people on the planet were potentially connected to the world's most popular social network in 2012.

With an increasing number of people using social networks such as Facebook, Google +, and Twitter, it's easier for people to stay connected with each other throughout the day. New technologies such as smartphones and tablets enable users to share photos, thoughts, and news articles with others instantaneously. Social media has revolutionized the ways in which we interact and share information with our peers, communities, colleagues, and the rest of the world.

For many people, social networks are simply thought of as Web sites that allow them to stay in touch with friends and family. But they go far beyond "likes" and retweets. Social networks make it possible for us to stay informed about what is happening in the lives of friends, family members, acquaintances, and classmates or colleagues. In the past, distances between people made it difficult to stay in touch on a regular basis. Today, social networks make it possible for us to maintain regular, active relationships with the people we care about. Instead of having to wait months for a family reunion to meet a newborn cousin or an aunt's new husband, for example, people are able to view, comment on, and share family photos and announcements much sooner.

It's not only our personal relationships and the way that we are able to stay connected that have been changed by social networks. Because of the ease and speed that information

Social Network-Powered Information Sharing

now travels through these channels, we are also able to stay informed about events occurring in our country and around the world before traditional news outlets, such as newspapers or television programs, are able to reach us. For instance, the 2012 London Olympics were often referred to as the "Twitter Olympics." This was because the results of many competitions spread through the microblogging Web site before they even aired on American and Canadian television channels.

Many businesses are taking notice of the potential benefits of using social networks as a way to market their services and

Japanese athlete Miyuki Maeda uses her smartphone during a badminton match at the 2012 London Olympics. News and match results were often spread through social networks before traditional media could reach audiences.

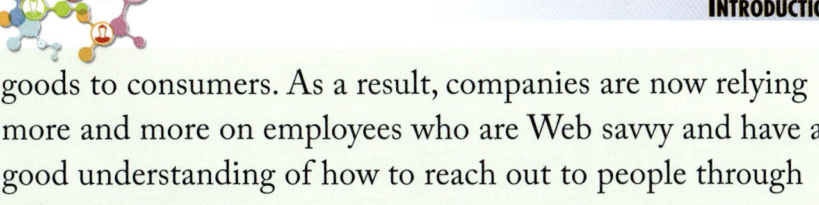

goods to consumers. As a result, companies are now relying more and more on employees who are Web savvy and have a good understanding of how to reach out to people through online interaction.

With all of the benefits of staying informed and connected online, however, it is also important to understand that there are potential downsides to using social networks. It is imperative to realize that how we interact on social networks today may affect us in the future, negatively or positively. How well social networks serve us depends upon how ethically, intelligently, and safely we conduct ourselves online.

Chapter 1

The Social Information Age

It is now hard to imagine living in a time before the Internet. For better or worse, the Web—and social networks in particular—have changed the way we communicate with each other and how we gather information about the world around us. Critics often argue that social networks have caused people to become withdrawn from one another in the offline world, creating a dependence upon technology to communicate and develop relationships. Proponents, however, might argue that social networks enable us to create and maintain relationships more easily. In addition, they provide us with access to an almost infinite amount of information that previous generations could not have possibly imagined.

Social networks, in many aspects, are still in a period of infancy. Society is still figuring out how to adapt to a technology that has opened a door to new opportunities for reaching out to each other. At the same time, that technology has closed the door on traditional methods of spreading and sharing information.

To gain a better idea of how social networks are changing the way we interact and spread and share information,

The Social Information Age

we need to first understand how they have evolved into the communication tools we now use on a daily basis.

Social Networking's Growing Pains

In 2002, computer programmer Jonathan Abrams founded Friendster, one of the first dedicated social networking sites to become successful. Members of the site were able to customize profiles to showcase photos, interests, and personal information such as birth dates and hometowns. However, it was the ease of being able to find and connect to friends and other users that helped the network obtain more than three million users within its first few months of going live.

Friendster's success, however, was short-lived. Competition from rival social networks such as Yahoo! 360, Windows Live Spaces, and MySpace gained larger audiences. This was because they provided users with more freedom to create and customize flashier profiles. These next-generation profiles included features such as music players and top friends lists.

Still, while these earlier social networks successfully figured out how to attract large numbers of users, they failed to encourage interaction between those members. As a result, their initial popularity faded over time. "Crafting a great profile can be fun, even satisfying," says PCMag.com writer Peter Pachal, "but it's really just another game. And like all games, it eventually bores you."

The early social networks created a space where people could find each other online. But further experimentation

Social Network—Powered Information Sharing

Jonathan Abrams became an early innovator of social networks when he launched Friendster in 2002. Despite a quick rise to popularity, Friendster eventually failed to compete against rivals MySpace and Facebook.

and learning from the failures of sites such as Friendster were required before developers could build sites that people would keep coming back to again and again.

To the initial dismay of many of its members, Facebook introduced a feature in 2006 called News Feed. Seen by many as a turning point in social networks, the new feature was a complete makeover of the Facebook homepage, which up until that point had been a customizable version of the user's profile. Upon logging into the social network, members were now shown a continually updating list of friends' activity on the site—a stream of information relating directly to the user and his or her friends. Facebook users now had a snapshot of what was currently happening in the lives of their network connections without necessarily having to visit their profiles individually. This made it possible for more people to engage in timelier discussions about information that was being shared.

The Top Three Information Hubs

The majority of people who use social networks regularly can be found on Facebook, Twitter, and Google +. These three networks appeal to broader audiences because they do not focus on a particular niche interest, as does a social networking site like HR.com, for example. HR.com is an online community for professionals in the human resources industry. Because they offer a common outlet for individuals with an extremely wide range of interests, the three leading social networks also provide the widest variety of information that is shared on social networks.

Google + and Facebook offer their members many similar features, such as private messaging, the ability for members to tag each other in posts and photos, and the ability to create groups. Since so many people use these two networks,

Social Network—Powered Information Sharing

INFORMATION SHARING OR LOSS OF PRIVACY?

When Facebook first introduced the News Feed, the company experienced a heavy backlash from members who felt that it had resulted in an invasion of their online privacy. Just about anything members posted, commented on, liked, or shared from other members could be seen by all of their connections. Subsequently, several online petitions and groups were formed, calling for the company to remove the new feature.

In an open letter to members, Facebook founder Mark Zuckerberg conceded that the company had failed to provide users with adequate privacy controls, saying: "We really messed this one up. When we launched News Feed and Mini-Feed, we were trying to provide you with a stream of information about your social world. Instead, we did a bad job of explaining what the new features were and an even worse job of giving you control of them."

As a result of the overwhelming criticism and irate complaints that the company received, privacy controls were added that gave users the option to limit the personal activity on the network that could be viewed by others. Over time, additional privacy settings have also

Facebook founder Mark Zuckerberg discusses the introduction of the social network's Time Line feature. Over the years, the company has regularly faced criticism regarding user privacy.

been introduced, including the ability to allow or prevent certain groups of connections from seeing the activity of a user. Still, Facebook is often accused of not taking enough steps to protect members' privacy and making it overly complicated to adjust privacy settings.

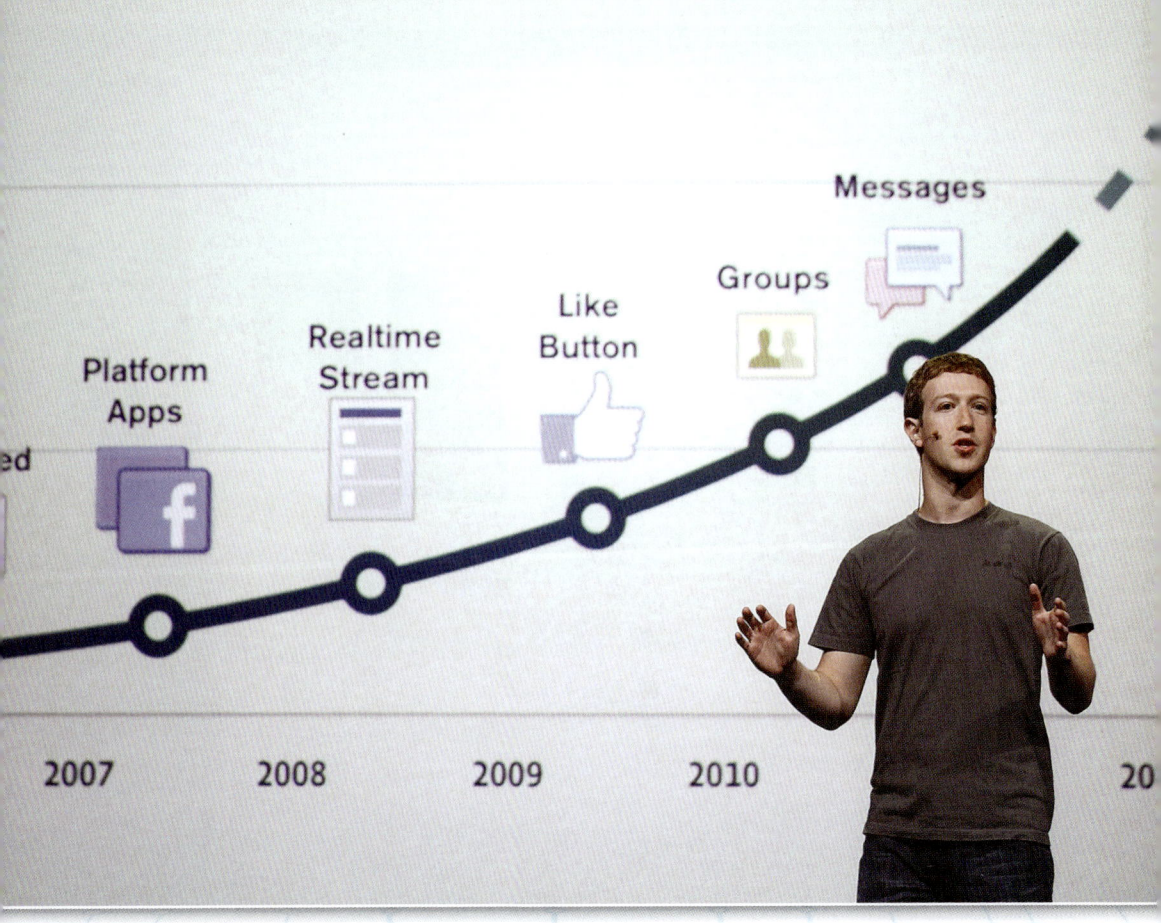

Social Network—Powered Information Sharing

they are prime communities within which to connect and share information with different groups of people.

Twitter has become one of the most popular social networks due to its relative ease of use, which can be attributed to its limited features. Adding to its appeal, many celebrities also have accounts, including singer Lady Gaga, who had more than thirty-five million followers by March 2013. According to the network's CEO Dick Costolo, Twitter users sent more than five hundred million tweets per day in 2012.

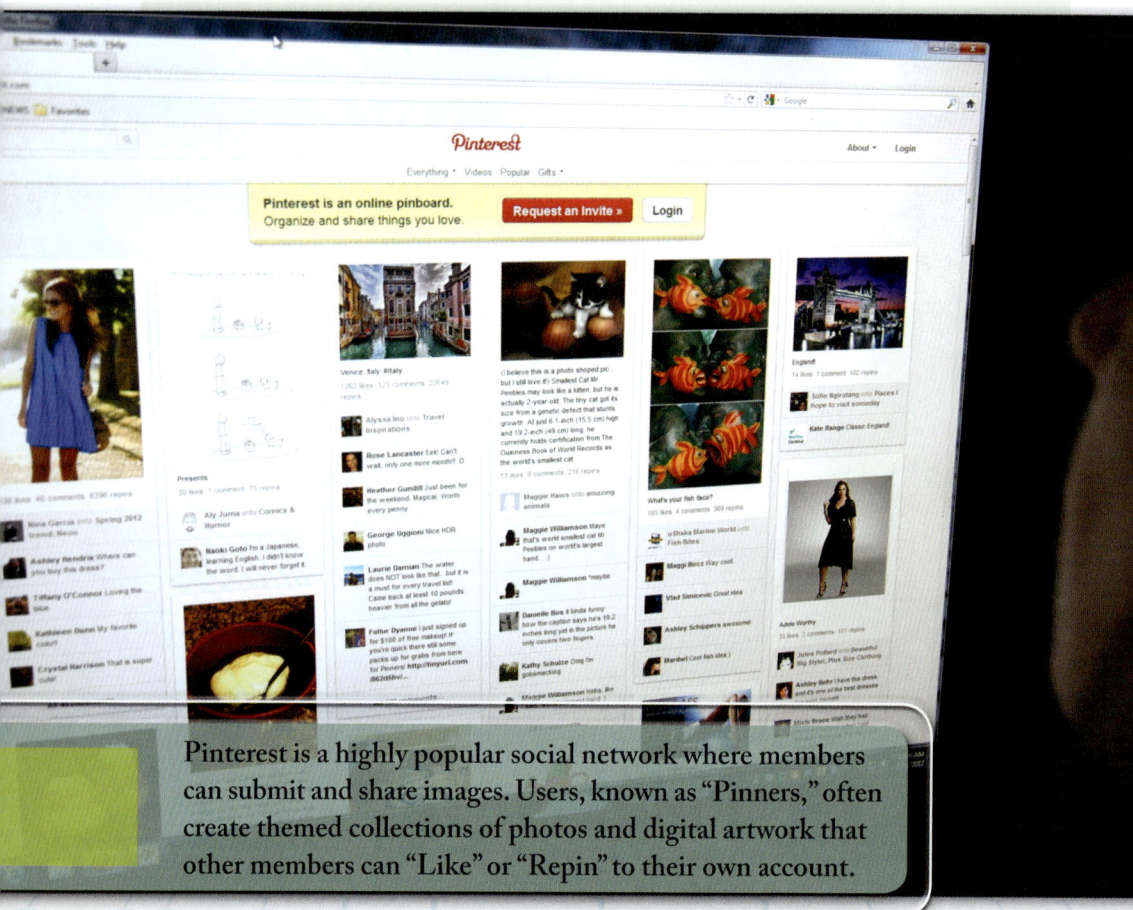

Pinterest is a highly popular social network where members can submit and share images. Users, known as "Pinners," often create themed collections of photos and digital artwork that other members can "Like" or "Repin" to their own account.

Even political leaders utilize social networks to connect with their constituents as a way to promote themselves, their causes, and the current issues to which they want to draw attention. Though he didn't have as many followers as Lady Gaga, President Barack Obama made social networking history after his 2012 reelection. Once he was declared the winner, he tweeted a photo of himself hugging First Lady Michelle Obama, along with the simple caption, "Four more years." His short message quickly became the most shared tweet, with more than eight hundred thousand retweets to date.

Niche Networks

One of the downsides of the more popular social networks is that they are not tailored to specific interest groups. Therefore, there is a good chance that if you are trying to get information across to like-minded individuals, the message may become buried in all the completely unrelated social chatter. To fill this gap, there are numerous social networks that cater to specific audiences.

Many of these niche networks offer the same functionalities as their major counterparts do, including the ability to leave messages on someone's profile, create and share photo albums, and engage in group discussions. The site deviantArt, for example, is a popular online community for artists that allows them to network, build portfolios, and showcase their work. This site allows artists to engage in discussions with fellow artists, art dealers and buyers, and art enthusiasts. By spreading their work among a community with a similar

Social Network–Powered Information Sharing

interest, members are able to increase the likelihood that their art could be noticed by gallery owners, potential buyers, and the art world press.

Social Media Sites

Whereas social networks function to connect people and generate interaction, social media Web sites offer a common space for users to find and share digital media. Pinterest, for instance, focuses solely on the sharing of images that mem-

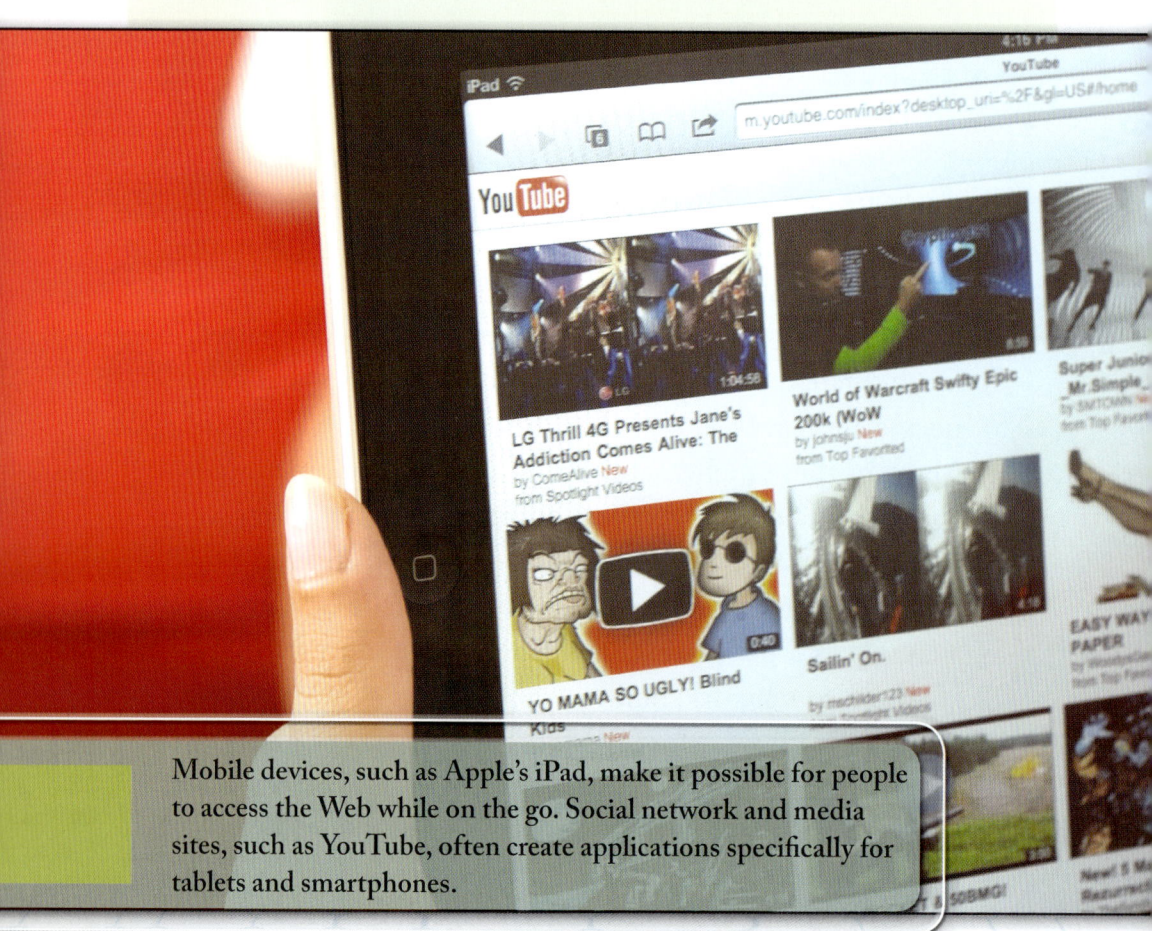

Mobile devices, such as Apple's iPad, make it possible for people to access the Web while on the go. Social network and media sites, such as YouTube, often create applications specifically for tablets and smartphones.

bers submit or post from around the Web. Pinners create and share photo boards that range in subject matter from wedding planning ideas and dinner recipes to vintage vinyl records and comic books.

The popular video-sharing site YouTube allows people to publically and privately post and discuss videos that can then be shared on social networks, blogs, and Web sites. According to the Web research company Alexa, YouTube was the third most visited site on the Internet in 2012, giving the video submissions of its users access to a large global audience.

Because of its popularity and the ability of some videos to go viral, several musicians and bands, who might have gone unnoticed otherwise, have gained large fan bases thanks to YouTube. These musicians and bands have even been signed to major record labels after having popular videos on the site. Justin Bieber, for instance, became an international success after his mom posted videos of his performances in 2007 that later caught the eye of R&B singer Usher. YouTube is similarly credited for the success of Carly Rae Jepsen, Gotye, OK Go, Psy, and Rebecca Black.

A Connected Web of Shared Information

In many cases, the sharing and spreading of information through social networks no longer requires an individual to be signed in at the site. Many Web sites now feature "sharing buttons" that allow visitors to post links to pages or articles directly onto their social networks with just one click of the mouse. The buttons, which are usually smaller versions of the social networks' logos, can be easily embedded into Web sites, including personal blogs. This inclusion of social network buttons on Web sites has become standard practice for individuals and organizations that want their content or message to be capable of being easily spread and seen by more people.

As the adoption of features such as sharing buttons works its way into the structure of Web sites, our ability to spread information across multiple social networks and to different audiences will become easier. This process of sharing pages and information to our social networks from across the Web also increases our potential to engage with others and generate discussions. For example, when someone clicks a Facebook "Like" button that is embedded in a page on a site such as CNN.com, other users in that individual's Facebook network will then be able to see the particular article the person has just viewed. They can then comment on, like, and even share the article among their own connections. These friends will then share the content with their other friends, and so on and so on. On a very large scale, this is how a piece of content—a photo, an article, a song, a video—can go viral.

To better illustrate how intertwined social networks have become with the rest of the Web in recent years and the enormous amount of information that is being spread and shared, consider the Google + button. It can be found on millions of Web pages and was used five billion times a day in 2012.

CHAPTER 2

Tracking the Local Scene

With the increased 24/7 access to online technologies and users' ability to get their information on the Web and through social networks, many traditional, local newspapers have been forced to shut down the printing presses for good. Even morning talk shows on the radio and evening news broadcasts on television are being increasingly tuned out and turned off. Once-loyal listeners and viewers can now pick from a wide variety of podcasts that they can quickly download or stream through iPods and smartphones. We are in the midst of a changing world for the local citizen—one where information about upcoming events, city council meetings, job ads, and local news stories is increasingly being gathered online.

Through social networks, you have the opportunity to become a model citizen in your own community. There are numerous ways in which you can harness your know-how and skills in spreading information through social networks to keep others informed about and actively involved in what really matters in your community.

Social networks and the technology you use on a daily basis can be used for personal entertainment and enjoyment, including podcasts and video chats. Additionally, you can use them to stay connected to and active within your community.

TRACKING THE LOCAL SCENE

Volunteering

In the past, charitable groups and community outreach organizations had to spend countless hours making phone calls and mailing costly appeal letters that, in many cases, would go ignored. The use of social networks can greatly reduce the amount of energy and resources that are required to spread information and reach out to the individuals who are most likely to give their time, money, and effort to such groups.

Mosaic Counseling and Family Services is an organization based in Kitchener, Ontario, Canada, that provides counseling and development programs for youths and adults. At one time, Mosaic workers and volunteers spent more than 3,600 hours annually reaching out to members by phone to give notification of upcoming events and schedule changes. Rather than actually communicating with members, much of this time was spent listening to ring tones, busy signals, and disconnected line messages, and the redialing of numbers. Realizing that people were spending more and more of their time online, particularly on Facebook and Twitter, the organization redirected its outreach efforts to social networks.

Using social networks as a communication tool paid off for the organization. "Utilizing social media has not only allowed our organization to better communicate and engage with our youth—it has also provided easier ways for our youth to communicate with us," specialty mentoring program facilitator Jason Shim told the Nonprofit Technology Network. "The switch has allowed staff in our program to spend more

Social Network–Powered Information Sharing

time focusing on building more positive relationships with our youth and less time listening to busy signals."

Social networks also help people find local organizations for which they are interested in volunteering. Many groups set up profiles on Facebook, Twitter, and Google +, making it easy for people living in the community to connect and stay informed of upcoming events and issues that they can participate in or help promote. Habitat for Humanity International, for instance, is a large volunteer organization that builds houses for people who have been left homeless as a result of natural

Organizations such as Habitat for Humanity International use social networks to reach out to potential volunteers. The Web makes it easier for such groups to keep members updated on organizational news and upcoming events.

disasters, war, poverty, and other dire situations. Many local chapters of the organization utilize Facebook profiles to spread information about upcoming building projects and ways that local citizens can contribute to Habitat-sponsored events in their own neighborhood.

Because so many young people spend time on social networks, they are also playing a large role in shaping the way volunteers and groups connect. In 2011, Priyanka Jain, then a seventeen-year-old Seattle, Washington, high school student, founded iCAREweCARE. This is the world's first social network dedicated to connecting high school and college-aged youth with organizations that depend on volunteers. "I began to notice how many students care about global issues but don't know what to do about it. I realized our generation has never had a platform where we can find opportunities to act locally with our friends, as well as engage in a global conversation about these problems," said Jain in an iCAREweCARE press release. "Community service is a meaningful experience that is much more fun and impactful when done with friends through social networks, and iCAREweCARE is the first nonprofit to encourage social change to be social."

The iCAREweCARE social network provides young people with an easy way to connect with each other, discuss their social concerns, and find volunteer projects within their community with which they can become involved. The social network also lets members share their experiences, both good and bad, so that others have a better understanding of how certain organizations operate. By being able to spread information about their volunteer experiences, iCAREweCARE

Social Network—Powered Information Sharing

HURRICANE SANDY'S FUEL SHORTAGE

In October 2012, Hurricane Sandy left a path of destruction across the Northeastern United States. Hundreds of thousands of people were left without power for weeks, homes and businesses were destroyed, and entire communities were nearly wiped off the map. In the wake of the storm's widespread damage, millions of motorists were forced to contend with a shortage of fuel. Lines at many gas stations that were able to remain open stretched for miles. On some occasions, people became confrontational with each other as a result of the stress. Many people drove long distances and even across state lines to obtain a commodity that is often taken for granted.

During the crisis, a group of students from Franklin High School in New Brunswick, New Jersey, took to the Web to help out their neighbors in need. Using the online mapping service Mappler, the students were able to identify and mark gas stations that had fuel. The group utilized information and messages posted on Twitter, Facebook, and media reports to locate where fuel was available.

Rather than driving around searching far and wide for fuel, drivers were able to simply check Mappler at home or from the road with their smartphones. The students' map also helped commercial and government efforts to identify where the fuel

Customers wait in line at a gas station in Brooklyn, New York, after Hurricane Sandy crippled the flow of oil in several states. Many people waited several hours in some locations, only to be turned away as pumps ran dry.

shortages were greatest and where to direct fuel resources during the crisis. "The experience has been a rollercoaster ride. I could have been playing video games, but instead I am helping to make a difference in this world. This project has united us all," said Josue Serrano, one of the students involved in the project (as quoted by Energy.gov).

members can help others decide whether or not a certain organization is trustworthy and worth giving their time to. It also allows people to evaluate if an organization is doing the kind of work that interests them and that they are capable of joining in and helping out with.

Bringing Small Businesses Online

In today's online-driven world, small businesses find themselves not only having to compete against superstores such as Wal-Mart and Target, but also against a customer base that increasingly prefers to do its shopping online. But this does not mean that small businesses are out of luck. Many business owners are successfully using social networks to reach out to their local communities and bring the customers back into the store.

Unlike much of today's youth, many small business owners are not tech savvy and are missing a great chance to encourage their businesses to thrive. One way you can help the businesses in your local community is by offering them your social networking experience. You can show business owners how to set up and maintain profiles on Facebook and how to connect to people who live and shop in the area. Pinterest is another great social network that retail businesses such as gift shops and florists can use to showcase their goods. Through the use of social networks, small businesses can stay connected to their community, notifying potential customers of discounts and promotional sales that can entice people to get offline and back on Main Street.

Rather than mowing lawns and raking leaves to earn money, some teens are becoming young entrepreneurs by capitalizing on their everyday use of social networks. In 2011, high school students Max Gardner, Brendan Reeve, and Louis Retief started their own social media management company, Plugged In, which specializes in boosting the online presence of small businesses. "Social media is such an important part of having a business today," Gardner told TheProgress.com. "You win if you know how to do it, and lose if you don't."

Having grown up with online resources such as social networks, e-mail, and Web sites, the three teens realized they could use their online skills to help local businesses spread information to their base of increasingly online customers. "If you grow up on a farm, you're going to be experienced at being a dairy farmer. And if you grow up living, breathing social media, you're going to be good at social media," said Gardner.

Social Networking Emergency Response

Instead of picking up the local newspaper to find out about upcoming events in their neighborhood, many people are now looking to their social networks to find out about what's happening around town. Local government institutions, such as chambers of commerce, use Facebook to inform citizens about grand openings of new businesses. Towns often create social network profiles to inform citizens about upcoming political meetings and publicize news and

Thousands of people were left without shelter and power after an earthquake struck Christchurch, New Zealand. Social networks made it possible for many victims to get in touch with loved ones and to stay informed of developing news.

announcements that directly affect their citizens, including construction plans, election dates, and school closings.

Mobile technology and social networks have proven to be an effective pairing of communication tools, making it possible to easily and quickly keep communities informed and alert during emergency situations. In 2011, a destructive 6.3 magnitude earthquake struck the city of Christchurch, New Zealand, leaving many residents without electricity. This essentially cut off access to information channels such as televisions, home phones, and radios that people have relied on in the past during disastrous situations.

However, through emergency planning, government staff used Twitter to send out more than five thousand tweets, spreading vital information to citizens who had access to mobile phones. "Many affected people did not have access to desktop computers, either at home or at work, but mobile data services remained available for many residents," Stephen Crombie, chief information officer for the New Zealand Police, told Mediabistro. "Twitter provided a mobile-friendly means of getting critical information out."

Another example of how the pairing of social networks and mobile technology is playing a role in the way local communities spread information is provided by a 2012 shooting at Chardon High School in Ohio that left three students dead and two others injured. As the event unfolded, several students at the school used their mobile phones to access Twitter and Facebook to notify parents and friends on the outside of what was happening. Many of the tweets and messages reported that gunshots were being heard in the school.

Social Network—Powered Information Sharing

As the situation came to an end, students tweeted to family and friends that they were unharmed. The situation at Chardon High demonstrated how powerful social networks can be at spreading information quickly during emergency situations when other communication channels to the outside are limited or nonexistent.

Spreading the Word of Local Change

Social networks allow people to connect online. As a result, they also provide a common outlet that citizens can use to discuss and express views on the issues that directly affect their community. Groups are often set up on Facebook to draw attention to and rally support around various causes of local concern. Issues can range from saving historical landmarks and requesting changes to local laws to calling for the recall of elected officials with whom voters are dissatisfied.

The beauty of social networks is that they make it easy for people of all ages to exercise their democratic right to have a say in how their government makes important decisions. This can be especially true for younger people who often feel that they have no say in the way the world around them is run.

In 2011, officials in Montgomery County, Maryland, proposed a curfew on anyone under eighteen. The curfew would ban teens from being in public places after 11:00 PM on weekdays and midnight on weekends. The proposal came as a result of several late-night incidents involving teens, one of which included a stabbing during a seventy-person

Tracking the Local Scene

altercation. The proposed curfew divided the community. Many people felt that a curfew would prevent area youth from getting in trouble. Opponents pointed out that past studies had proven curfews to be an ineffective mechanism for social control and law and order.

Many young people and other opponents of the law in Montgomery County felt that a curfew would be an unjust punishment against law-abiding youth who would suffer because of the misdeeds of a small minority of troublemakers. As a result, the Facebook group "Stand Up to the MoCo

Young people can use social networks to bring attention to the issues they care about. Creating a group on a social network is a great way to connect with others who care about the same causes.

Social Network–Powered Information Sharing

Youth Curfew!" was launched. Information about the campaign quickly spread, and the group gained nearly two thousand members in opposition to the proposal. "It's so much more than a group of kids complaining about the curfew," Alan Xie, a student and coorganizer of the Facebook campaign told the *Bethesda Patch*. "It's a group of kids organizing themselves to do something about it."

As the campaign's popularity grew and word spread through social networks, the National Youth Rights Association, an organization that works with students to fight government-imposed curfews, lent its support. Eventually, as a result of the negative public attention and growing opposition, local lawmakers scrapped the curfew proposal. By utilizing social networks to rally together and spread information about the issues affecting the community and its youth, students are proving that they not only have a voice, but they also have real social and political power and influence.

CHAPTER 3

Information Sharing's Impact upon Journalism, Public Health, and Public Debates

The information sharing made possible by social media technology has radically transformed society, revolutionizing the practice of journalism, extending the reach of public health initiatives, and amplifying the volume and passion of public debates.

Social Networks: First on the Scene

Shortly after 11:30 PM on May 1, 2011, President Obama announced to the American television audience that the world's most wanted terrorist, Osama bin Laden, had been killed by a team of U.S. Navy Seals in Abbottabad, Pakistan. In actuality, though, Obama was not the first person to break the news to the world.

Social Network–Powered Information Sharing

As the president was preparing his announcement speech that night, Twitter was already buzzing with speculation. Rumors of bin Laden's death quickly gained momentum after Keith Urbahn, the former chief of staff for Donald Rumsfeld, the secretary of defense under President George W. Bush, sent out a tweet. In his message, which was posted an hour before the president spoke on national television, Urbahn wrote, "So I'm told by a reputable person [that] they have killed Osama Bin Laden..."

In 2009, Janis Krums was the first to break news of the "Miracle on the Hudson," an incident in which a US Airways flight made a safe emergency landing on New York City's Hudson River. From a ferry on the river, Krums tweeted a photo she took with her smartphone. It showed passengers standing on the wings and inflatable emergency slide of the half-submerged plane, with the caption: "There's a plane in the Hudson. I'm on the ferry going to pick up the people. Crazy."

Information Sharing's Impact upon Journalism, Public Health, and Public Debates

Armed with mobile technology and a Twitter account, Krums spread the captivating news before television networks and news organization Web sites.

People no longer have to turn on the television to catch breaking news. In 2009, news of an emergency landing of a passenger flight on the Hudson River in New York City was first reported on Twitter, well ahead of the television and cable news networks, wire services, and print and radio news media.

SOCIAL NETWORK–POWERED INFORMATION SHARING

Citizen Journalism: Promise and Peril

Today, it's not that uncommon for traditional news outlets to be late to the party when it comes to breaking news first. The ability of citizens to spread information through social networks before journalists are able to provide coverage and analysis can be extremely beneficial, especially during emergency situations. However, it is also important to emphasize that not everything you read on Twitter or Facebook is true.

Unlike mainstream media, tweets and posts—examples of so-called citizen journalism—are not fact-checked, nor do they contain expert analysis. They are simply in-the-moment accounts of what may be happening. As such, they are completely subjective and liable to be tainted by exaggeration, rumor, inaccuracy, misunderstanding, and an incomplete and biased perspective.

In addition, there are people who use social networks to purposely spread false information and rumors. Unlike newspapers and television news networks that rely on fact checkers and editors to verify reports, social networks are breeding grounds for the spread of false and damaging information that can have incredibly dangerous and volatile real-world effects. "The problem with social media or the Internet is how quickly this information can spread," said social psychologist Aleks Krotoski in an interview with BBC News. "Misinformation has been around for a really long time, but historically there have been gatekeepers to confirm things externally."

Information Sharing's Impact upon Journalism, Public Health, and Public Debates

For example, news of a 2011 riot in London, England, quickly spread across Twitter. While riots had broken out in a specific neighborhood, several people intentionally began spreading rumors that civil unrest had broken out across other parts of the city. The false information forced many shopkeepers to close up early, thinking looters were striking their neighborhood. Many residents spent the night in fear, while public officials tried to restore calm by ascertaining what was actually happening and where it was happening.

Misinformation, rumors, and false news on social networks can create problems in the offline world. In 2011, the extent of riots in a London suburb were exaggerated online, resulting in panic and economic losses in unaffected areas of the city.

37

Social Network–Powered Information Sharing

As is the case with anything found online, it's always good practice to make sure that the source of information is reliable (such as the Web site of a reputable news organization) before forming an opinion and spreading potentially deceptive and false news to others.

Information Goes Viral

Social networks are used by organizations to spread information about health crises around the world. Through social media, health organizations can raise both awareness and funds that can be used to prevent and fight devastating diseases and illnesses that threaten the world population.

The World Health Organization (WHO) is an agency of the United Nations that focuses on international public health. WHO connects with citizens around the world through social networks to raise public awareness about potential health threats and quickly spread information that could save lives during medical and other emergencies.

After Japan was hit by a devastating tsunami in 2011 that caused a radiation crisis at a nuclear plant in the city of Okuma, WHO analyzed communication on social networks to monitor resulting potential health problems. Reports began to emerge that some people were drinking chemicals that contained iodine, which is thought to protect people from radiation. WHO immediately took to Twitter and Facebook to warn people against self-medicating and drinking such products because they could cause more harm than good.

INFORMATION SHARING'S IMPACT UPON JOURNALISM, PUBLIC HEALTH, AND PUBLIC DEBATES

MALARIA NO MORE

In 2009, actor Ashton Kutcher joined forces with Malaria No More, an organization that raises awareness about malaria. This is a deadly mosquito-borne disease that affects billions of people across the planet and is responsible for up to one million deaths annually. Via social networks, Kutcher and other celebrities have been able to reach out to millions of people to raise money to help fight the preventable illness. Through their efforts on social networks, Malaria No More has been able to deliver life-saving education, medication, and mosquito nets to the international communities that are most vulnerable.

These individuals use a GPS system to track and report malaria outbreaks. Social networks allow organizations to raise awareness of potential outbreaks of disease across the world.

Shaping the Debate and Testing Freedoms

In the fight for civil rights in the United States throughout the 1950s and 1960s, activists participated in mass marches and sit-ins to show solidarity against laws they felt were discriminatory and unconstitutional. After much bloodshed, violence, and tears, the civil rights movement did prove successful at reshaping the way the country treated minorities and guaranteed their liberties.

While public protests for and against laws and pressing social issues still exist today, the debates that lead to changes in the system are also taking place across social networks. This forces officials to pay more attention to issues that are causing a stir online.

In the wake of the 2012 shooting massacre at Sandy Hook Elementary School in Newton, Connecticut, which

Information Sharing's Impact upon Journalism, Public Health, and Public Debates

claimed twenty-seven lives, people across the United States took to social networks to voice their disgust and shock about what had happened. Amid the tweets and status updates

Proponents of stricter gun control laws march across the Brooklyn Bridge in New York City in the wake of the Sandy Hook shootings. Rallies and protests such as this one are often organized via social networks.

41

CHAPTER 4

The Global Town Square

As social networks change the way information travels throughout your community, they are also having a profound impact across the entire planet. The way we perceive and communicate with our neighbors next door and halfway around the world has rapidly become more transparent as globalization and technology push us closer together. This has radically altered the ways in which we experience, think about, and respond to issues relating to international affairs, immigration, trade, war, and human rights. With technologies such as Facebook's translation tool, which allows users to read translations of foreign language texts on the social network, the ability to spread information between people of different nations and languages is just a click away.

In some cases, this worldwide spread of information has helped achieve positive changes in society by bringing people together who were previously divided by history, culture, language, politics, religion, and geography. Still, there are parts of the world where the available lines of communication through the Web and social networks have been tightly controlled. This has limited their freedom to spread information and gain knowledge, a freedom that

THE GLOBAL TOWN SQUARE

many people around the world now take for granted as a basic right and privilege.

Following @Gov

Ordinary citizens are not the only ones who are taking to social networks to inform and be informed. Heads of governments and political leaders around the world are also utilizing these channels of communication to help gauge

Governments and politicians are increasingly turning to the Web and social networks as a way to communicate with citizens.

Social Network–Powered Information Sharing

and influence public opinion on important matters of national and global interest. From small-town mayors to the presidents and leaders of nations, it seems that everyone has found his or her way onto Twitter and Facebook.

Whether or not the leaders and governments that tweet and post status updates are well-meaning or ill-intentioned toward their citizens, neighbors, and the international community as a whole is up for debate. The fact of the matter is that many politicians and world leaders have realized the power that the Web offers when it comes to rallying support among citizens and framing their positions in the best possible light. And because they occupy leadership positions in society, they are generally held in high regard and people may be more apt to believe the messages they share.

@CHAVEZCANDANGA

Before his death in March 2013, the president of Venezuela, Hugo Chavez, was considered by many to be one of the most charismatic leaders in recent history. As part of that

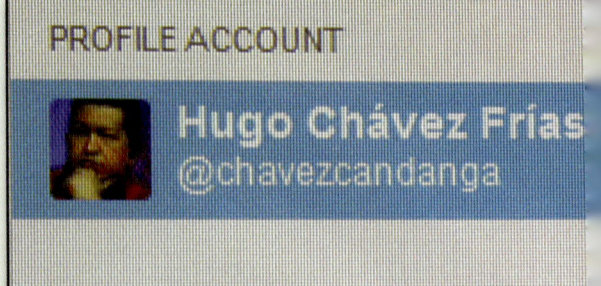

Former Venezuelan president Hugo Chavez initially condemned social networks as a threat to society. His viewpoint eventually changed as he utilized the networks to spread his own political ideology and propaganda.

dynamic outreach, he embraced the use of media as a mouthpiece for spreading political ideology.

For years, Chavez hosted a weekly talk show that was broadcast on Venezuela's state television and radio stations. As social networks came into popularity in nations such as the United States (a nation he often clashed with), Chavez initially condemned them stating, "The Internet is a battle trench because it is bringing a current of conspiracy" (as quoted by the *Guardian*). Eventually, realizing that social networks offered a new way to reach and influence people, he joined Twitter. Chavez even hired a team of two hundred aides to help him manage his account, which eventually amassed more than four million followers.

Hugo Chávez Frías @chavezca · 3h
Sigo aferrado a Cristo y confiado en mis médicos y enfermeras. Hasta la victoria siempre!! Viviremos y venceremos!!!

Hugo Chávez Frías @chavezca · 3h
Gracias a Fidel, a Raúl y a toda Cuba!! Gracias a Venezuela por tanto amor!!!

Hugo Chávez Frías @chavezca · 3h
Hemos llegado de nuevo a la Patria venezolana. Gracias Dios mío!! Gracias Pueblo amado!! Aquí continuaremos el tratamiento.

Social Network—Powered Information Sharing

Through social networks, Chavez was able to spread his socialist ideas, while also demonizing political opponents and Western nations. In 2010, he even went so far as to encourage his supporters to use social networking sites as a tool to attack his opponents. In particular, he targeted students who used Facebook and other online tools to plan protests against his government.

@DalaiLama

Tenzin Gyatso, known as His Holiness the 14th Dalai Lama, was only fifteen years old when he became the leader of Tibet in 1950. In 1959, the Dalai Lama was forced into exile in India after the government of China refused to acknowledge his authority over Tibet, a nation that it considered to be subject to its own rule. Decades later, however, many people living in Tibet and followers of Tibetan Buddhism around the world still refer to the Dalai Lama as the leader of the Tibetan government-in-exile.

Embracing the Internet as a useful and vital tool to facilitate communication with his followers, the seventy-seven-year-old spiritual leader has profiles set up on several social networks, including Twitter, Facebook, YouTube, and Google +. Millions of people are connected to the Dalai Lama, retweeting and sharing his messages on a daily basis.

In 2011, the Dalai Lama was scheduled to appear with South African social rights activist and Anglican bishop Desmond Tutu to celebrate the former apartheid opposition leader's eightieth birthday and to discuss their shared interest in social justice. However, the Dalai Lama was denied entry into South Africa because of visa issues that some speculated were the result of intervention by the Chinese government. While the two leaders were unable to join together in person to discuss the issues closest to their hearts, they instead utilized Google+'s video chat feature called Hangouts. This allowed people from across the world to tune into a live, streaming discussion between the two statesmen.

The Viral Information Campaign

On March 5, 2012, the organization Invisible Children released the short film *Kony 2012* on video-sharing sites such as YouTube and Vimeo. The film was made as a global call to action to capture the infamous African militia leader Joseph Kony, who had been accused of ordering his rebel fighters to abduct children and force them to carry arms. The film obtained the support of celebrities such as George Clooney and Oprah Winfrey. They, in turn, publicized the video through their own social networks that consisted of millions of followers, and the video quickly went viral worldwide. According to a poll by the PEW Research Center, nearly 60 percent of American youths were aware of the Kony movement within just a few days of the film's release.

As a result of calls for action from citizens across the United States, President Obama ordered the deployment of one hundred special forces to aid African Union soldiers in

SOCIAL NETWORK–POWERED INFORMATION SHARING

Supporters of the Kony 2012 campaign participate by placing posters in public areas to raise awareness. The campaign's social network strategy involved help from celebrities and reached millions of people around the world.

50

The Global Town Square

tracking down Kony in Uganda, where he was thought to be hiding. The campaign also helped Invisible Children raise millions of dollars from supporters. Unfortunately, even with all the publicity that was gained, Kony remained at large.

Tweetin' About a Revolution

Since December 2010, many Middle Eastern nations have experienced a rise in political upheaval and protests known collectively as the Arab Spring. Leaders in Tunisia, Libya, Yeman, and Egypt have been forced from power after clashes between citizens and government forces turned deadly, and, in some cases, resulted in foreign military intervention. One factor that has been debated is the role that social networks played in sparking these civil uprisings.

According to a March 2011 poll released by the Dubai

Social Network—Powered Information Sharing

School of Government, close to nine out of ten Egyptians and Tunisians were using Facebook as a tool to organize protests and spread information about the uprisings. At the same time, one of the most frequently used Twitter hashtags was #protest, underscoring the type of information that was being shared. During the uprisings, many governments attempted to prevent citizens from accessing social networks. However, just over a quarter of people reported that the efforts had prevented them from being able to organize. Many people said that the attempts to block communication actu-

In the Middle East, social networks were used by citizens to organize protests during the Arab Spring movement. Several governments, including those of Libya, Egypt, and Tunisia, collapsed as a result of the civil unrest.

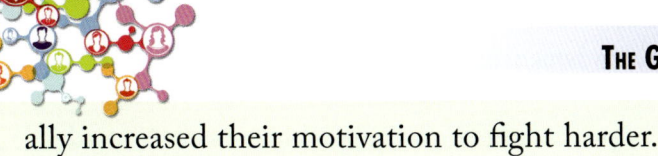

ally increased their motivation to fight harder.

Whether or not it can be proven that social networks actually ignited the uprisings in the Middle East by giving people an outlet for venting their frustrations with their governments, they have undeniably been important weapons for the coordination and spreading of information, opinions, and action.

Social Network Blackouts and Censorship

Many nations do not allow citizens to practice freedom of speech. In some countries, speaking out against laws and policies or criticizing the government and its leaders can result in harsh punishments. These can include fines, jail time, or even execution. Before the widespread use of the Internet, it was easier for regimes to control channels of communication, such as television, newspapers, and radio stations.

Today, however, dictatorships and other authoritarian governments are forced to contend with the worldwide online networks that allow large numbers of people to instantaneously and somewhat anonymously spread and share information, opinions, and strategies threatening to the powers that be.

Iran

In the case of Iran, the Internet was initially as unrestricted and open to users as it currently is in most Western nations. However, as activists began using it as a forum to speak out against the repressive religious government, restrictions

Social Network–Powered Information Sharing

were increasingly put in place and punishments were made harsher. In 2009, during a period of civil unrest known as the Iranian Green Movement, many citizens used Facebook and Twitter to plan mass protests. They were reacting against a presidential election that they felt had been rigged in favor of the incumbent conservative president Mahmoud Ahmadinejad.

As a result of the protests that often turned into violent clashes between citizens and security forces, the regime tightened its monitoring of social networks and online activity. One law that was passed requires that Internet service providers (ISPs) store user data for a minimum of three months, giving government agencies ample time to sift through user activity and identify the "troublemakers."

CHINA

Rather than restricting the use of social networks such as Facebook, Twitter, and Foursquare, the government of China allows its mainland citizens to only use approved social networks, which are tightly monitored and filtered for specific content. The most popular social network in China is Renren. It is essentially a knockoff of Facebook. Weibo is another popular network, modeled after Twitter.

Online anonymity in China is also a target of government disdain. In 2011, the government announced that users of Weibo would have to use their real names rather, than online handles. However, the policy never went into effect. When enforcement of the law didn't take place, many online users joked about it. As a result, the government required

The Global Town Square

Weibo to censor posts that contained phrases such as "real name registration."

Known as "the Great Firewall of China," the government requires ISPs to block access to numerous popular Web sites, including YouTube, Google, and most social networks that are based in other nations. The prevention of access to certain sites on the Web can severely limit the type of information

Chinese citizens are only allowed to use social networks that have been approved by the government. This woman is using Weibo, a popular Chinese network that is modeled after Twitter.

the experience of feeling accepted, which they might not be able to do among their offline peers.

Building large networks of connections and developing relationships with others online can create a sense of inner satisfaction. In too many cases, however, the satisfaction is often short-lived, as the true nature of the individual on the other side of the screen emerges or the lack of privacy becomes too intrusive or even threatening.

Amanda Todd, a teenager from Canada, became a victim of online and offline bullying after becoming too trusting of a stranger she met while video chatting. The individual later posted a topless photo of Todd on the Internet. Fearing that her peers would find out about the photo, Todd began having anxiety and panic attacks. As a result, her parents moved to another city where she could attend another school.

Safe Information Sharing Today and Tomorrow

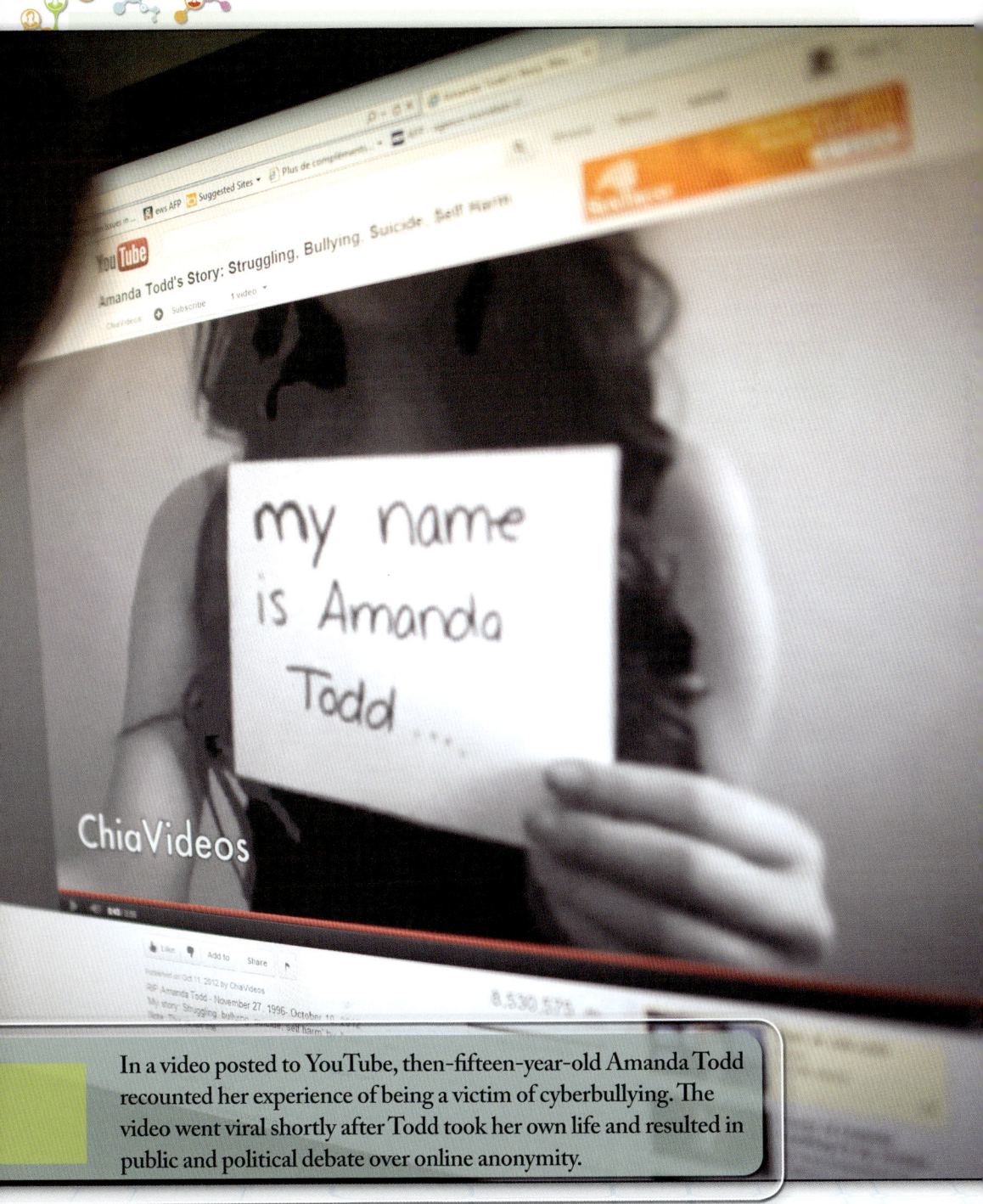

In a video posted to YouTube, then-fifteen-year-old Amanda Todd recounted her experience of being a victim of cyberbullying. The video went viral shortly after Todd took her own life and resulted in public and political debate over online anonymity.

Social Network—Powered Information Sharing

Unfortunately, Todd's online past continued to haunt her. Her cyberbully created a Facebook account under her name using the topless photo as the profile image. He then connected to students from her new school. Having seen the compromising photo, they, in turn, relentlessly teased and bullied Todd. After multiple suicide attempts and a transfer to several different schools, Todd's relentless online bully continued to stalk and intimidate her through social networks. He connected with her peers wherever she went, spreading the information from which she had tried so hard and for so long to escape.

In October 2012, after years of deepening depression and emotional trauma, Todd took her own life. Todd's case exemplifies the danger of being too trusting of online strangers. It also shows how our online activity and what we share with others can find its way onto social networks, even if we didn't put it there to begin with.

Think Twice Before You Post

The oversharing of personal problems and the venting of frustrations via social media can often backfire. In the heat of the moment, people turn to social networks to voice their anger and frustration. When friends or followers learn what is happening in your life, they can then share that information among their own connections, sparking rumors that can be personally damaging. You lose control of the message once it slips past your trusted circle of friends. Before taking to social networks to share personal problems, frustrations, or other information, take a moment to consider your content. It is always wise to take a moment to consider if what you are sharing is something that others could somehow use against you. This includes photos, videos, and personal identifying information like addresses, credit card numbers, and phone numbers.

Safeguarding Against Information Thieves

Other problems that have developed as a result of the sharing of personal information on social networks are identity theft and financial fraud. Because social networks offer access to so many people's personal lives, tech–savvy criminals are now utilizing these channels to gather sensitive information. They can then use this information to set up credit cards, take out loans, and withdraw money from banking accounts. This is a particularly alarming problem for younger people because they often do not fully realize the extent of the damage that can be done by sharing basic information such as birth dates, employment history, and phone numbers.

According to *PC World*, more than one-third of users on social networks share at least three pieces of personal information that identity thieves can take advantage of. Additionally, nearly 60 percent of social networkers do not know to what degree of security their privacy controls are set. To decrease the risk of becoming a victim of identity theft, avoid sharing your full name, birth date, address, telephone numbers, and names of family members. Also,

Social Network–Powered Information Sharing

WHEN SHARING BACKFIRES

In January 2013, the social news site Reddit was abuzz over a receipt for a meal at an Applebee's restaurant that was posted by waitress Chelsea Welch. The receipt included an automatically added 18 percent tip that Alois Bell, a local pastor, felt was unnecessary. Instead of paying the tip or talking to a manager, Bell wrote on the receipt, "I give God 10 percent" and "Why do you get 18?" In place of the asked tip amount, she added "0."

The posted receipt quickly gained attention from Reddit users, many of whom criticized Bell's response. Soon, news sites such as the *Huffington Post* and Yahoo! News featured the trending story on their front pages. When a friend told Bell that she had made the front page of Yahoo!—but not for the most flattering of reasons—she got in touch with Welch's manager. Subsequently, Applebee's fired Welch because she had violated a customer's right to privacy by posting the photo of the restaurant bill. "I had no intention of starting a witch hunt or hurting anyone. I just wanted to share a picture I found interesting," Welch told Yahoo! News. "I come home exhausted, sore, burnt, dirty, and blistered on a good day. And after all that, I can be fired for 'embarrassing' someone who directly insults their server on religious grounds."

One's history of comments posted to social networks is not easily erased and can result in real-world problems. Most social networks feature privacy controls that allow you to decide who can see your interactions.

Safe Information Sharing Today and Tomorrow

Stories such as Welch's are not uncommon. Many employers pay attention to the activity of their employees on social networks. Complaining about bosses, customers, and jobs online or engaging in discussions or activities that could reflect poorly on a company can often result in the receiving of a pink slip.

Sharing on Facebook

These settings control who can see what you sha[re]

Everyone

Friends of friends

Friends only

Social Network–Powered Information Sharing

read privacy agreements, only "friend" people you know and trust, and research online how to adequately manage the privacy settings of each social network you use.

When creating a social network account, avoid providing the company with information that others could figure out by looking at your profile. When setting up an account, many Web sites ask for answers to personal questions that can be used to reset a forgotten password. For example, sites often ask for the name of a first pet or favorite schoolteacher. Without thinking about the possible repercussions, people

Identity theft and fraud are serious dangers for people who use the Web and social networks. Be very careful when giving out personal information, including credit card numbers. Only give this information to trusted and legitimate online retailers.

post these names in common discussions on social networks. Individuals could then use that information to gain access to accounts by resetting passwords. Instead of providing real names to such questions, give fake answers that can be easily remembered, and always use different passwords for each Web site that requires them.

Tweeting to Your Future Self

As students prepare for their next steps toward adulthood, social networking and online activity play a role in how young people are perceived by authority figures. Colleges and employers often use social networks to identify promising individuals who can contribute to and improve their organizations. Our actions and the information we share on social networks act as digital footprints that people can use to gauge personality traits such as responsibility, restraint, respect of others, and work ethic. It's important to grasp this concept at a young age because it is often difficult, and, sometimes impossible, to erase or cover up digital footprints later on.

The Online Admissions Office

According to a 2011 Kaplan Test Prep survey, nearly 25 percent of university and college admissions officials conducted background research on applicants by looking them up on

Social Network—Powered Information Sharing

Facebook and Google. Considering that in 2008 only 10 percent of those surveyed researched students online during the admissions process, the analysis of social media activity is becoming an important method of learning more about applicants and their behavior and attitudes.

There is no certainty regarding how an admissions officer might factor a student's posted history on social networks into the decision-making process. But there is the very real possibility that an inappropriate photo or an off-color joke could be held against you and disqualify you from further consideration. "Maybe it is a little unfair, but at the same time, you're being judged on what you have created for yourself in the past four years of your high school experience," Maxton Thoman, a freshman at the University of Alabama, told *Time* magazine. "All that stuff is cumulative, and so is Facebook."

So, how can a student begin preparing to apply to schools? For one, be wary of the photos and information you share. Avoid posting and being tagged in pictures that could show a lack of judgment. Colleges and universities set high academic and behavioral expectations because their students represent the schools and the values they hold. "We have seen students who have been involved in bullying behavior or alcohol or drugs," Martha Blevins Allman, dean of admissions at Wake Forest University, told the *Wall Street Journal*. "We never use it as a single indicator, and we don't search blindly, but if we have other suspicions, we will look."

Yes, admissions officials are paying more attention to social networks, but there are many benefits to being active on them. Don't hesitate to share accomplishments and activities that could reflect well on a school application. Show support for the college you hope to attend by joining its official Facebook group or connecting to it via Twitter, Google+, or LinkedIn. Simple interactions such as commenting on and sharing photos and articles posted to a college's social network profile can display your sincere interest in the school to an admissions officer.

Who Checks the Classified Ads Anymore?

Employers are scouring social networks and the Web to determine if potential employees fit their ideal of the perfect employee. At the same time, they are utilizing social networks to publicize job opportunities. In essence, the Web and social networks are replacing the classified ads in newspapers that past generations used to find work.

One of the most popular social networks for finding a job out of high school or college is LinkedIn. The network is aimed at connecting working professionals, businesses, and job seekers. The site requires individuals to be at least eighteen years old before joining. Upon creating an account, users can showcase their résumé and talents, search for suitable job openings, and network with others.

Many companies that utilize social networks are also looking for tech-savvy individuals who know how to market themselves in a professional light and can successfully disseminate information through the Web. It's vitally im-

Social Network–Powered Information Sharing

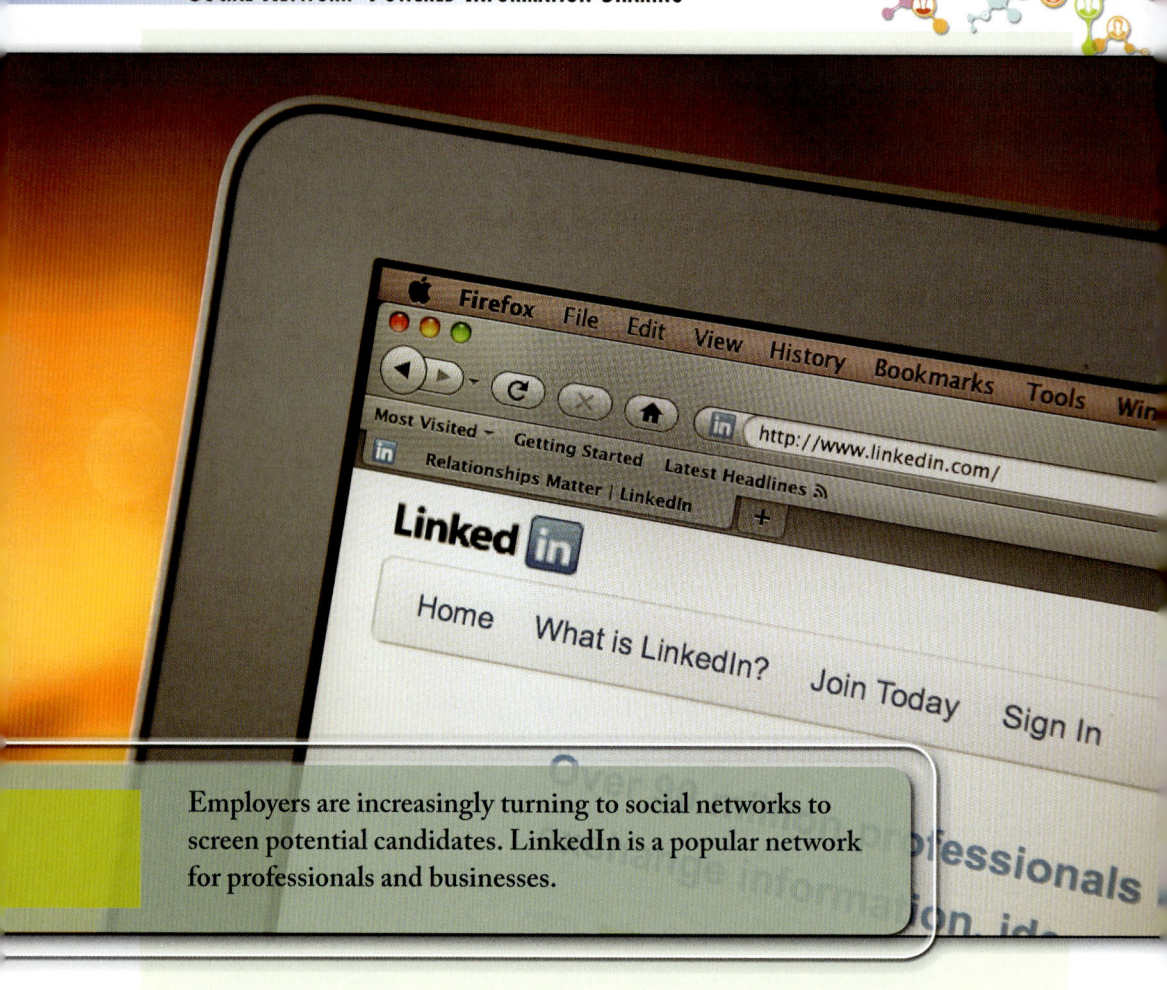

Employers are increasingly turning to social networks to screen potential candidates. LinkedIn is a popular network for professionals and businesses.

portant to understand how to manage your online presence through social networks by filtering the information you share and how you share it. This can make all the difference years down the road, as people who have some influence over your future trace the digital footprints of your past.

GLOSSARY

channel A medium used for communication or the passage of information.

commodity A raw material that is in demand.

constituent A member of a community or organization who has the right to vote during elections and is represented by elected officials.

disseminate To spread or disperse information.

exile To be away from one's home or country by choice or because one is denied the right to return.

globalization The process whereby different regions and countries become integrated through mutually used networks of communication, transportation, and trade.

handle A nickname used in online communication.

ideology A system of ideas that forms the basis of political beliefs.

Internet service provider (ISP) A business or organization that provides customers with access to the Internet.

intertwine To become involved or bound inextricably together.

niche A highly specific, specialized, and targeted topic.

podcast Video or audio program, similar to a radio show, that is distributed through the Internet.

portfolio A collection of someone's creative work that is used to display his or her skills.

relentless Describes the act of continuing or persisting in doing something without considering or caring about the consequences.

remote feed The streaming of live video or audio to viewers across the Internet.

repercussion The consequence or effect of an action or decision.

Socialist An individual who advocates a political theory that states that the means of production, distribution, and exchange should be regulated by the government.

stream A continuous flow of information.

tagging Identifying or marking an individual or place in a social network message or photo, thereby associating that person with the posted material.

viral Describes when an image, video, message, or other form of information and media is rapidly circulated on the Internet.

FOR MORE INFORMATION

Electronic Frontier Foundation (EFF)
454 Shotwell Street
San Francisco, CA 94110–1914
(415) 436–9333
Web site: http://www.eff.org
The EFF provides legal expertise and advocacy for consumers and the general public in an effort to curb violations of freedom of speech, the right to information, and privacy on the Internet. The nonprofit organization provides legal representation and support for individuals and groups that have been victims of online privacy invasion and monitoring by the U.S. government and large corporations.

MediaSmarts
950 Gladstone Avenue, Suite 120
Ottawa, ON K1Y 3E6
Canada
(613) 224–7721
Web site: http://www.mediasmarts.ca
This organization strives to increase the digital and media literacy skills among Canadians through educational resources and programs that promote critical thinking and use of online resources, including social networks and news obtained from the Web. The organization's mission is to develop engaged, informed, and active citizens.

National Coalition Against Censorship (NCAC)
19 Fulton Street, Suite 406
New York, NY 10038
(212) 807-6222
Web site: http://www.ncac.org
The NCAC is an alliance of fifty-two organizations that is dedicated to protecting freedom of expression and access to information. The organization works to expand public awareness of censorship and suppression of information and provides educational and advocacy support to individuals and groups that are victims of censorship.

OpenMedia.ca
1424 Commercial Drive
P.O. Box 21674
Vancouver, BC V5L 5G3
Canada
Web site: http://www.openmedia.ca
OpenMedia.ca engages, informs,

Social Network—Powered Information Sharing

and empowers citizens to protect their communication rights through online campaigns, events, and educational resources. The organization advocates for the right to access high-speed communications such as the Internet and the freedom to access the Web without content gatekeepers and government censorship.

PACER's National Bullying
Prevention Center
8161 Normandale Boulevard
Bloomington, MN 55437
(800) 537-2237
Web site: http://www.pacer.org
PACER's National Bullying Prevention Center unites, engages, and educates communities nationwide to address bullying through creative, relevant, and interactive resources.

Privacy International
46 Bedford Row
London, WC1R 4LR
England
Web site: http://www
.privacyinternational.org
Privacy International is an organization that raises awareness and monitors reports of unlawful surveillance and violations of privacy by governments and corporations.

Social Media in Organizations
1530 South State Street, #925
Chicago, IL 60605
(312) 225.3365
Web site: http://www.sminorgs
.net
Social Media in Organizations focuses on how social media will impact employees and organizational functioning, as well as general social and economic trends.

Web Sites

Due to the changing nature of Internet links, Rosen Publishing has developed an online list of Web sites related to the subject of this book. This site is updated regularly. Please use this link to access the list:

http://www.rosenlinks.com
/TGPSN/Info

FOR FURTHER READING

Andrews, Lori. *I Know Who You Are and I Saw What You Did: Social Networks and the Death of Privacy.* New York, NY: Free Press, 2012.

Castells, Manuel. *Networks of Outrage and Hope: Social Movements in the Internet Age.* Cambridge, England: Polity, 2012.

Christakis, Nicholas A., and James H. Fowler. *Connected: The Surprising Power of Our Social Networks and How They Shape Our Lives—How Your Friends' Friends' Friends Affect Everything You Feel, Think, and Do.* New York, NY: Back Bay Books, 2011.

Contreras, Esteban. *Social State: Thoughts, Stats, and Stories About the State of Social Media in 2013.* Vancouver, BC, Canada: Social Nerdia, 2013.

Dulworth, Michael. *The Connect Effect: Building Strong, Professional, and Virtual Networks.* San Francisco, CA: Berret-Koehler Publishers, 2008.

Gleick, James. *The Information: A History, a Theory, a Flood.* New York, NY: Vintage Books, 2012.

Howard, Philip N., and Muzammil M. Hussain. *Democracy's Fourth Wave?: Digital Media and the Arab Spring* (Oxford Studies in Digital Politics). New York, NY: Oxford University Press, 2013.

Jenkins, Henry, Sam Ford, and Joshua Green. *Spreadable Media: Creating Value and Meaning in a Networked Culture.* New York, NY: NYU Press, 2013.

Keen, Andrew. *Digital Vertigo: How Today's Online Social Revolution Is Dividing, Diminishing, and Disorienting Us.* New York, NY: St. Martin's Press, 2012.

MacKinnon, Rebecca. *Consent of the Networked: The Worldwide Struggle for Internet Freedom.* New York, NY: Basic Books, 2012.

Masum, Hassan, and Mark Tovey, eds. *The Reputation Society: How Online Opinions Are Reshaping the Offline World*

(The Information Society). Cambridge, MA: MIT Press, 2012.

Newsom, Gavin, and Lisa Dickey. *Citizenville: How to Take the Town Square Digital and Reinvent Government.* London, England: The Penguin Press HC, 2013.

Qualman, Erik. *Socialnomics: How Social Media Transforms the Way We Live and Do Business.* Hoboken, NJ: Wiley Publishing, Inc., 2010.

Rainie, Lee, and Barry Wellman. *Networked: The New Social Operating System.* Cambridge, MA: MIT Press, 2012.

Sinclair, Betsy. *The Social Citizen: Peer Networks and Political Behavior* (Chicago Studies in American Politics). Chicago, IL: University of Chicago Press, 2012.

Stearman, Kaye. *Freedom of Information* (Ethical Debates). New York, NY: Rosen Publishing, 2011.

Van Dijk, Jan. *The Network Society.* 3rd ed. Thousand Oaks, CA: Sage Publications, 2012.

Watkins, S. Craig. *The Young and the Digital: What the Migration to Social Network Sites, Games, and Anytime, Anywhere Media Means for Our Future.* Boston, MA: Beacon Press, 2010.

Wilkinson, Colin. *Mobile Platforms: Getting Information on the Go* (Digital and Information Literacy). New York, NY: Rosen Publishing, 2011.

Wilkinson, Colin. *Twitter and Microblogging: Instant Communication with 140 Characters or Less* (Digital and Information Literacy). New York, NY: Rosen Publishing, 2011.

BIBLIOGRAPHY

Bartel, Katie. "Chilliwack Teens Start Social Media Business." *Chilliwack Progress*, January 9, 2012. Retrieved February 2013 (http://www.theprogress.com/community/136960878.html).

Belkin, Douglas, and Caroline Porter. "Web Profiles Haunt Students." *Wall Street Journal*, October 4, 2012. Retrieved February 2013 (http://online.wsj.com/article/SB10000872396390443768804578035500956712628.html).

Carrero, Jacquellena. "New Jersey Student Leads Gas Station Mapping Project in Sandy's Wake." *NBC Latino*, November 3, 2012. Retrieved February 2013 (http://nbclatino.com/2012/11/03/new-jersey-student-leads-gas-station-mapping-project-in-sandys-wake).

Carrol, Rory. "Hugo Chavez Embraces Twitter to Fight Online 'Conspiracy.'" *Guardian*, April 28, 2010. Retrieved February 2013 (http://www.guardian.co.uk/world/2010/apr/28/hugo-chavez-twitter-venezuela).

Catone, Josh. "How Social Media Helped 174 Million People Get the Message About Malaria." Mashable.com, September 20, 2010. Retrieved March 2013 (http://mashable.com/2010/09/20/social-media-malaria).

Deards, Helena. "Twitter First Off the Mark with Hudson Plane Crash Coverage." World Association of Newspapers and News Publishers, January 1, 2009. Retrieved February 2013 (http://www.editorsweblog.org/2009/01/19/twitter-first-off-the-mark-with-hudson-plane-crash-coverage).

Dugan, Lauren. "Twitter Used as Impromptu Emergency Broadcast System During Ohio School Shooting." MediaBistro.com, February 28, 2012. Retrieved February 2013 (http://www.mediabistro.com/alltwitter/twitter-used-as-impromptu-emergency-broadcast-system-during-ohio-school-shooting_b19030).

Handley, Ann, and C. C. Chapman. *Content Rules: How to Create Killer Blogs, Podcasts, Videos, Ebooks, Webinars (and More) That Engage Customers and Ignite Your Business.* Hoboken, NJ: Wiley, 2012.

Haven, Stephanie. "Students Rally Online Against Curfew." *Bethesda Patch,* July 14, 2011. Retrieved February 23, 2013 (http://bethesda.patch.com/articles/montgomery-county-students-petition-proposed-curfew).

Honigman, Brian. "100 Fascinating Social Media Statistics and Figures from 2012." *Huffington Post,* November 29, 2012. Retrieved February 2013 (http://www.huffingtonpost.com/brian-honigman/100-fascinating-social-me_b_2185281.html).

Jackson, Peter. "England Riots: Dangers Behind False Rumours." BBC News, August 11, 2011. Retrieved February 2013 (http://www.bbc.co.uk/news/uk-14490693).

Kanczula, Antonia. "Kony 2012 in Numbers." *Guardian,* April 20, 2012. Retrieved February 2013 (http://www.guardian.co.uk/news/datablog/2012/apr/20/kony-2012-factsnumbers?newsfeed=true#zoomed-picture).

Luckerson, Victor. "When Colleges Look Up Applicants on Facebook: The Unspoken New Admissions Test." *Time,* November 15, 2012. Retrieved February 2013 (http://nation.time.com/2012/11/15/when-colleges-look-up-applicants-on-facebook-the-unspoken-new-admissions-test).

Mansfield, Heather. *Social Media for Social Good: A How-to Guide for Nonprofits.* New York, NY: McGraw-Hill, 2011.

Marya, Radhika. "Dalai Lama Joins Google+, Plans Hangout with Desmond Tutu." Mashable.com, October 7, 2011. Retrieved March 2013 (http://mashable.com/2011/10/07/dalai-lama-desmond-tutu-google-plus).

Bibliography

Merrill, Douglas C., and James A. Martin. *Getting Organized in the Google Era: How to Stay Efficient, Productive (and Sane) in an Information-Saturated World.* New York, NY: Crown Business, 2011.

Olson, David. "WHO Finds Social Media Indispensable in Managing Health Crises." *Huffington Post*, May 21, 2012. Retrieved March 2013 (http://www.huffingtonpost.com/david-j-olson/who-social-media_b_1530016.html).

Pachal, Peter. "Why Friendster Died: Social Media Isn't a Game." *PC Magazine*, April 28, 2011. Retrieved February 2013 (http://www.pcmag.com/article2/0,2817,2384588,00.asp).

Shim, Jason. "From Phones to Facebook: How to Engage Youth on the Front Lines of Social Media." Nonprofit Technology Network, January 19, 2012. Retrieved February 2013 (http://www.nten.org/articles/2012/from-phones-to-facebook-how-to-engage-youth-on-the-front-lines-of-social-media).

Smith, Catharine. "Osama bin Laden's Death Leaked via Twitter." *Huffington Post*, July 1, 2011. Retrieved February 2013 (http://www.huffingtonpost.com/2011/05/02/osama-bin-laden-death-twitter-leak_n_856121.html).

Tabin, Herbert, and Craig Agranoff. *Checked-In: How to Use Gowalla, Foursquare, and Other Geo-Location Applications for Fun and Profit.* Deerfield Beach, FL: Pendant Publishing, 2010.

Terdiman, Daniel. "Report: Twitter Hits Half a Billion Tweets a Day." CNET.com, October 26, 2012. Retrieved February 2013 (http://news.cnet.com/8301-1023_3-57541566-93/report-twitter-hits-half-a-billion-tweets-a-day).

Van Dijck, Jose. *The Culture of Connectivity: A Critical History of Social Media.* New York, NY: Oxford University Press, 2013.

INDEX

A
Arab Spring, 51–53

B
bin Laden, Osama, 33–34

C
censorship, 53–56
Chardon High School shootings, 29–30
Chavez, Hugo, 46–48
China, 48, 49, 54–56
Christchurch earthquake, 29
citizen journalism, reliability of, 36–38
college admissions, 65–67
cyberbullying, 57–60

D
Dalai Lama, 48–49
deviantArt, 15
disease and illness prevention, 38–39

E
emergency response, 27–30
employment ads and Web sites, 67–68

F
Facebook, 4, 18, 22, 24, 26, 27, 29, 30, 31–32, 36, 38, 44, 46, 48, 52, 54, 60, 66, 67
  News Feed, 10–11, 12–13
Friendster, 9, 10

G
global politics and social networking, 46–49, 51–56
Google, 4, 11, 18, 22, 48, 49, 55, 66, 67
gun control, 42–43

H
Habitat for Humanity International, 22–23
HR.com, 11

I
iCAREweCARE, 23, 26
Iran, 53–54

J
Japan tsunami (2011), 38

K
Kony, Joseph, 49–51

L
LinkedIn, 67
local government and community concerns, 27, 30–32
London Olympics (2012), 6

M
malaria, 39
Mappler, 24–25
"Miracle on the Hudson," 34–35
Montgomery County curfew controversy, 30–32

INDEX

Mosaic Counseling and Family Services, 21
MySpace, 9

N

national politics and social networking, 45–46, 49–51
National Youth Rights Association, 32

O

Obama, Barack, 15, 33, 42, 49

P

Pinterest, 16–17, 26
Plugged In, 27

R

real-time reporting, 33–35
Reddit, 62

S

Sandy, Hurricane, 24–25
Sandy Hook Elementary shootings, 40–42
sharing buttons, 17–18
small businesses, 26–27
social debate, using social networks to foster, 40–43
social media sites, 16–17

social networking
  and digital footprints, 65–67
  history of, 9–10
  and identity theft, 61, 64–65
  niche sites, 11, 15–16
  and oversharing, 60–61
  overview of three largest sites, 11, 14–15
  privacy violations, 12–13
  pros and cons, 8

T

Todd, Amanda, 58–60
Twitter, 4, 11, 14–15, 22, 24, 29, 34, 35, 36, 37, 38, 46, 47, 48, 52, 54, 67

V

volunteering, 21–23, 26

W

Windows Live Spaces, 9
World Health Organization, 38

Y

Yahoo!360, 9
YouTube, 17, 48, 49, 55

Z

Zuckerberg, Mark, 12

About the Author

Joe Greek is a writer from Tennessee who has written for business and tourism publications. He currently lives in New York, where he works for a publishing company.

Photo Credits

Cover, p. 4 © iStockphoto.com/Robert Churchill; cover, pp. 1, 8, 19, 33, 44, 57 (background icons) © iStockphoto.com/Matt Chalwell; p. 1 © iStockphoto.com/frankreporter; pp. 4 (background), 5 © iStockphoto.com/Danil Melekhin; pp. 6, 10, 24–25, 50–51 © AP Images; pp. 12–13, 68 Justin Sullivan/Getty Images; p. 14 Karen Bleier/AFP/Getty Images; p. 16 © iStockphoto.com/Hocus Focus Studio; p. 20 ImagesBazaar/Getty Images; p. 22 Joe Raedle/Getty Images; p. 28 Fairfax Media/Getty Images; p. 31 Marili Forastieri /Digital Vision/Getty Images; pp. 34–35 Sharkpixs/ZUMA Press /Newscom; p. 37 Leon Neal/AFP/Getty Images; p. 39 Karen Kasmauski/Science Faction/SuperStock; pp. 40–41 Spencer Platt /Getty Images; p. 45 Aaron Ontiveroz/Denver Post/Getty Images; pp. 46–47 AFP/Getty Images; p. 52 Joel Carillet/E+/Getty Images; p. 55 Mark Ralston/AFP/Getty Images; pp. 58–59 Mladen Antonov/AFP/Getty Images; p. 63 © iStockphoto.com/Sam Burt Photography; p. 64 Jupiterimages/Brand X Pictures/Thinkstock; additional design elements © iStockphoto.com/P2007 (social networking icons), © iStockphoto.com/imagotres (network illustration).

Designer: Nelson Sa; Photo Researcher: Karen Huang